SPECIAL OLYMPICS

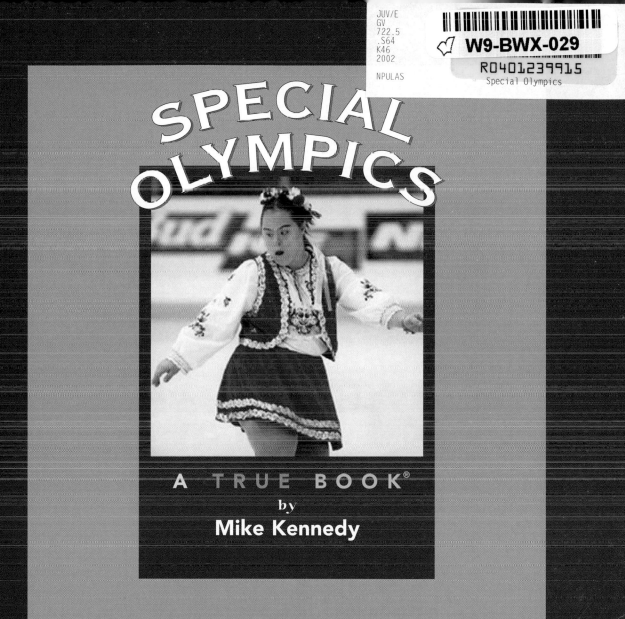

A TRUE BOOK®

by
Mike Kennedy

Children's Press®
A Division of Scholastic Inc.

New York Toronto London Auckland Sydney
Mexico City New Delhi Hong Kong
Danbury, Connecticut

A Special Olympics athlete competing in the shot put

Reading Consultant
Nanci R. Vargus, Ed.D.
Teacher in Residence
University of Indianapolis
Indianapolis, Indiana

The photograph on the cover shows a Special Olympics athlete receiving a medal. The title page shows a Special Olympics ice-skating competition.

Library of Congress Cataloging-in-Publication Data

Kennedy, Mike (Mike William), 1965-
    Special Olympics / by Mike Kennedy.
        p. cm. – (A true book)
    Includes bibliographical references and index.
    Summary: Gives a brief history of Special Olympics, athletic competition for people with mental retardation, and describes some of the events and how the games are run.
    ISBN 0-516-22338-0 (lib. bdg.)   0-516-29375-3 (pbk.)
    1. Special Olympics—Juvenile literature. [1. Special Olympics.] I. Title.
II. Series.

GV722.5.S64 K46 2002
796.04'56—dc21
                                                                    2001047201

Contents

The Opening Ceremonies of the Special Olympics Massachusetts Summer Games in 2001

Let the Games Begin

Is anything more exciting than athletic competition? Baron Pierre de Coubertin did not think so. He lived in France in the late 1800s and was part of a new generation that loved sports. Amazingly, just a century before, sports were thought to be a waste of time and energy. By Coubertin's **era**, however, people had come to appreciate the importance of physical fitness.

Coubertin was one of many who wanted to find a way to celebrate all the good things about sports. He suggested that the world's best athletes gather every four years for a series of competitions. His idea was based on the ancient games of Greece held in the valley of Olympia thousands of years earlier. The modern

Baron Pierre de Coubertin (right) and a track event at the first modern Olympic Games, in Athens in 1896 (below)

"Olympic Games" were born. The first competition took place in the summer of 1896.

In the years that followed, the Olympics gained in significance. Women began to compete in 1900. The first Winter Games occurred in 1924. Being selected to host the Games became a great national honor. By 1960, the Olympics had grown into the world's most exciting sporting event.

A woman named Eunice Kennedy Shriver watched this with great interest. She was a member of one of the most famous families in the United States. In fact, her

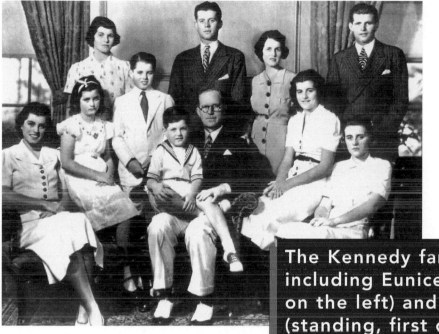

The Kennedy family in 1938, including Eunice (seated, first on the left) and Rosemary (standing, first on the left)

brother John Fitzgerald Kennedy was elected president in 1960.

Shriver had always wanted to make life better for people with mental retardation. One of her sisters, Rosemary, had been born with mental retardation.

The first Special Olympics Games, in Chicago in 1968 (above), and Eunice Kennedy Shriver holding a special coin honoring her work with Special Olympics (right)

The challenges her sister faced made Shriver think: Why not give people with mental retardation a chance to show their abilities in a competition like the Olympics? In 1968, she organized the first International Special Olympics Summer Games at Soldier Field in Chicago, Illinois. Approximately 1,000 athletes competed in three events: athletics, floor hockey, and aquatics.

From there, Special Olympics spread quickly around the world. People with mental retardation loved the chance to enjoy sports. Volunteers from all walks of life offered their assistance and

An athlete lights the flame at the start of a Special Olympics competition in Louisiana.

learned to value each person's abilities.

Today, nearly one million athletes from 160 countries participate in 26 sports in Special Olympics Programs around the globe. The two biggest events are the World Summer Games and World Winter Games, each

Today, athletes from all over the world participate in a wide variety of Special Olympics events.

held once every four years. No matter what the level of competition, however, Special Olympics lets people with mental retardation demonstrate their abilities.

What is Mental Retardation?

Mental retardation means that a person learns more slowly than other people his or her age. Some people are born with mental retardation and others develop it in

The athletes who compete in Special Olympics have mental retardation.

childhood. It is not a disease, a physical problem like a broken bone, or a mental illness that needs to be controlled with medicine or counseling.

Mental retardation affects the way a person lives, works, and plays. People with mental retardation may find it difficult to do things related to learning that come naturally to other people. They might not be able to solve math problems or read this book. They might have trouble communicating

with others, taking care of themselves, or living on their own. They may or may not also have physical disabilities.

There are more than 170 million people around the world with mental retardation, and each is an individual with his or her own set of talents, abilities, and disabilities. You interact with them every day, often without realizing it. In most ways, they are not different from you. If family and friends give them a chance, people with mental retardation can live successful, productive lives.

People with mental retardation can live successful and productive lives.

Golden Opportunities

Long before Special Olympics
athletes advance to the World
Games, they compete in local
events. These competitions are
held in towns and cities across
the United States and through-
out the world. They take place
at elementary schools, YMCAs,
and gyms. Athletes who do

A long jumper
stretching for
a little extra
at a local
Special Olympics
competition

well at local events qualify for
higher levels of competition.
Ultimately, the lucky ones move
on to the World Games.

A Special Olympics volunteer celebrates with a young athlete at a Special Olympics state bowling tournament.

Special Olympics athletes may compete in as many sports as they choose. Of course, they are limited some-what by the weather where they live. For example, it might be hard for someone in hot and sunny Florida to find a way to practice snow skiing. Athletes are required to train

The 100-meter cross-country skiing competition is one of many cold-weather Special Olympic sports.

for 8 weeks during the year. Coaches trained and approved by Special Olympics often oversee their workouts.

In competition, athletes are divided into groups called divisions based on age, ability, and gender. That means children never go up against adults. It also means that everyone has an equal chance to win.

For example, there could be several different divisions in a swimming event for teenagers. Each division would have

In Special Olympics, athletes of similar age and ability compete against each other.

between three and eight competitors who are very close in age and ability.

Each division crowns its own champions. The top finisher in each division receives a gold

Special Olympics champions are awarded medals (above) or ribbons (right).

medal or blue ribbon, the second-place finisher a silver medal or white ribbon, and the third-place finisher a bronze medal or yellow ribbon. The other participants in the division also receive ribbons for their efforts.

Local events lead to area or regional events, and then to state or national events. In every case, only medal winners advance to the state or national level, where the whole divisioning process begins again.

A local-level Special Olympics softball game

If Special Olympics athletes are competing in a year when the World Games are not being held, earning a state or national medal is the highest honor they can receive. In years when the World Winter or Summer Games are being held, gold medalists have a chance to move on to represent their national Special Olympics Program at a world event.

Not every champion, however, goes to the next level.

Those lucky enough to make it to the World Games (above) relish the chance to go for the gold (right).

To determine who does, Special Olympics requires each country or U.S. state Program to conduct a "lottery." That means that athletes who won gold medals at the National Games are selected by drawing names out of a hat. Those lucky enough to be chosen have the opportunity of a lifetime. They try to bring home the gold.

It is important to remember that the Special Olympics World Games are not the world championships of Special Olympics. The World Games are a chance for Special Olympics athletes of all abilities from all over the world to show their love of sports.

The Special Olympics World Games draw athletes from all over the world, including such places as Ivory Coast (top), the Isle of Man (bottom left), and the Netherlands (bottom right).

Let It Snow

The first snowflakes of winter are always special. But they are extra-special for Special Olympics athletes. The arrival of cold weather means these athletes can start practicing even harder for the World Winter Games.

Perhaps no one loves to see winter arrive more than

Champion skier and snowboarder Christopher Vance (left) helped bring the sport of snowboarding (above) to Special Olympics.

Christopher Vance, an avid skier and snowboarder. He has participated in Special Olympics since 1987, and has competed in the World Winter Games three times.

Several years ago, Christopher **lobbied** for his favorite sport, snowboarding, to become an official Special Olympics event. Christopher got enough people to listen, and Special Olympics decided to evaluate snowboarding to make sure it met the organization's requirements. Today Special Olympics athletes everywhere are trying this fun and challenging sport.

Although Special Olympics does not keep records, Mark Barber is considered one of the world's fastest Special Olympics speed skaters. Since

1985, he has earned more than 60 gold medals in this sport. In fact, at the 2001 World Winter Games, Mark swept the 777-meter, 1,000-meter, and 1,500-meter events.

Though they compete in the winter, athletes such as Christopher and Mark must train year-round to stay in top shape. That is because sports such as snowboarding and speed skating require tremendous balance and **stamina** as well as near-perfect technique.

Special Olympics Winter Sports

Special Olympics offers training and competition in the following winter sports:

- Alpine skiing
- Cross-country skiing
- Figure skating
- Floor hockey
- Snowboarding
- Snowshoeing
- Speed skating

Figure skating

Floor hockey

Speed skating

Snowshoeing

Fun in the Sun

Like the World Winter Games, the World Summer Games are held once every four years, with a full schedule of events at the local, state, and national levels in between.

These days, Cindy Bentley knows how to make the most of her summers. But there was a

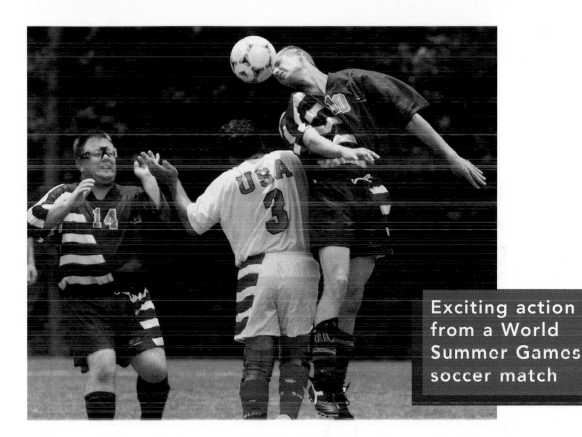

time when fun was something only other kids seemed to have. As a child, she was shuffled through **foster care**. Later, she was placed in a center for people with **developmental disabilities**.

Today, Cindy Bentley is an international spokesperson for Special Olympics.

But Cindy never gave up. She got involved in Special Olympics more than 10 years ago and has since earned medals in six summer events: basketball, athletics, volleyball, soccer, softball, and tennis. In 1991, Cindy was selected as the U.S. Female Special Olympics Athlete of the Year.

Today, Cindy lives on her own in Wisconsin and serves on the Special Olympics Wisconsin Board of Directors and as a Governor's appointee to the state Council on Developmental Disabilities.

Courage is a quality shared by Michael Rosario. He has competed in cycling, bowling, basketball, athletics, and **equestrian** events. He also represented North Carolina on Team USA in the 1999 World Summer Games, and won gold and silver medals. A former champion high-school wrestler, he

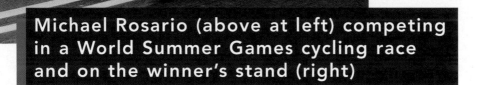

Michael Rosario (above at left) competing in a World Summer Games cycling race and on the winner's stand (right)

has been honored as his school's Best Student Athlete and as the Special Olympics North Carolina Athlete of the Year. Michael's greatest honor, however, was being awarded the United States Air Force's Silver Medal of Valor after he saved the life of a young girl at a water park.

Special Olympics Summer Sports

Special Olympics offers training and competition in the following summer sports:

- Aquatics
- Athletics
- Badminton
- Basketball
- Bocce
- Bowling
- Cycling
- Equestrian sports
- Football (Soccer)
- Golf
- Gymnastics (Artistic and Rhythmic)
- Powerlifting
- Roller skating
- Sailing
- Softball
- Table tennis
- Team handball
- Tennis
- Volleyball

Equestrian

Gymnastics

Powerlifting

Team handball

Volleyball

In Good Hands

Special Olympics has become a great way for people with mental retardation to enjoy all the benefits of sports. They improve their physical fitness. They experience the thrill of competition. They learn how much it takes to go for a goal that is hard to reach. And they make friends that last a lifetime.

Athletes from Finland wave to the crowd during the opening ceremonies of the 1999 Special Olympics World Summer Games in Raleigh, North Carolina.

Those friends include the people who enthusiastically volunteer their time to Special Olympics in more than 20,000 local meets and tournaments each year. Among the millions who offer their support with training, **promoting**, **officiating**,

Athletes, coaches, friends, and family members all have fun at Special Olympics events.

and cheering are people from your state, your town, and perhaps even your block.

All of these people are happy to help out, and they do so for the same reason. They want to work hard, have fun, and share the passion, pride, and joy with

42

these wonderful athletes. They also discover something they may not have expected. For a group of people labeled as "slow learners," Special Olympics athletes have a lot to teach the world about attitude, bravery, and always trying your best.

At Special Olympics competitions, people make friendships that last a lifetime.

To Find Out More

Here are some additional resources to help you learn more about Special Olympics and people who have mental retardation:

 **Books**

Brown, Fern G. **Special Olympics** (First Books). Franklin Watts, 1992.

Brown, Tricia. **Someone Special Just Like You.** Owlet, 1995.

Froese, Mary Frances. **Heroes of a Special Kind.** Evergreen Publications, 1999.

Gilbert, Nancy. **The Special Olympics.** Creative Education, 1989.

McNey, Martha, and Leslie Fish. **Leslie's Story: A Book About a Girl with Mental Retardation.** Lerner Publications Company, 1996.

Pulver, Robin. **Way to Go, Alex.** Albert Whitman, & Company, 1999.

Shriver, Maria. **What's Wrong with Timmy?** Warner Books and Little, Brown, and Company, 2001.

💡 Organizations and Online Sites

All Kids Can
http://www.allkidscan.org
Find out how you can participate in the All Kids Can Project, a disabilities awareness program in which you can discover new friends, develop new ideas, and learn more about people with disabilities through class projects.

Kids Together, Inc.
http://www.kidstogether.org
Provides information and resources for children and adults with disabilities.

Special Olympics
http://www.specialolympics. org
Official site of Special Olympics. Includes links to many other informative sites.

Important Words

developmental disability disability that causes a person to have trouble in at least three of the following areas: learning, language, self-care, getting around, and supporting oneself

equestrian related to horseback riding

era time period

foster care when the government appoints someone to care for a child other than his or her biological parents

generation group of people born during the same period in history

interact to communicate with someone

lobbied influenced someone

officiating overseeing as a referee

promoting spreading the news about someone or something

stamina ability to do an activity for a long period of time

Index

(**Boldface** page numbers
indicate illustrations.)

Meet the Author

Mike Kennedy is a freelance sportswriter whose work has ranged from Super Bowl coverage to historical research and analysis. He has profiled athletes in virtually every sport, including Peyton Manning, Bernie Williams, and Allen Iverson. He is a graduate of Franklin & Marshall College in Lancaster, Pennsylvania.

Mike has contributed his expertise to such books as *Auto Racing: A History of Fast Cars and Fearless Drivers*. He has authored four other True Books, including *Basketball* and *Football*.